Natural Disasters

Earthquakes

by Julie Murray

3

Dash!
LEVELED READERS
An Imprint of Abdo Zoom • abdobooks.com

3 Dash!
LEVELED READERS

Level 1 – Beginning
Short and simple sentences with familiar words or patterns for children who are beginning to understand how letters and sounds go together.

Level 2 – Emerging
Longer words and sentences with more complex language patterns for readers who are practicing common words and letter sounds.

Level 3 – Transitional
More developed language and vocabulary for readers who are becoming more independent.

THIS BOOK CONTAINS RECYCLED MATERIALS

abdobooks.com

Published by Abdo Zoom, a division of ABDO, PO Box 398166, Minneapolis, Minnesota 55439.

Printed in the United States of America, North Mankato, Minnesota.
052024
092024

Photo Credits: Getty Images, Shutterstock
Production Contributors: Kenny Abdo, Jennie Forsberg, Grace Hansen, John Hansen
Design Contributors: Candice Keimig, Neil Klinepier

Library of Congress Control Number: 2023948513

Publisher's Cataloging in Publication Data

Names: Murray, Julie, author.
Title: Earthquakes / by Julie Murray
Description: Minneapolis, Minnesota : Abdo Zoom, 2025 | Series: Natural disasters | Includes online resources and index.
Identifiers: ISBN 9781098285517 (lib. bdg.) | ISBN 9781098286217 (ebook) | ISBN 9781098286569 (Read-to-me eBook)
Subjects: LCSH: Natural disasters--Juvenile literature. | Earthquakes--Juvenile literature. | Seismology--Juvenile literature. | Geodynamics--Juvenile literature.
Classification: DDC 904.5--dc23

Table of Contents

Earthquakes

Earthquakes cause the ground to move. This can be a shaking-back-and-forth or rolling motion. Earthquakes occur on land and in the ocean floor.

Thousands of earthquakes occur around the world every year. Most are small enough that they are not felt. Others are powerful. These can lead to a natural disaster.

Tectonic Plates

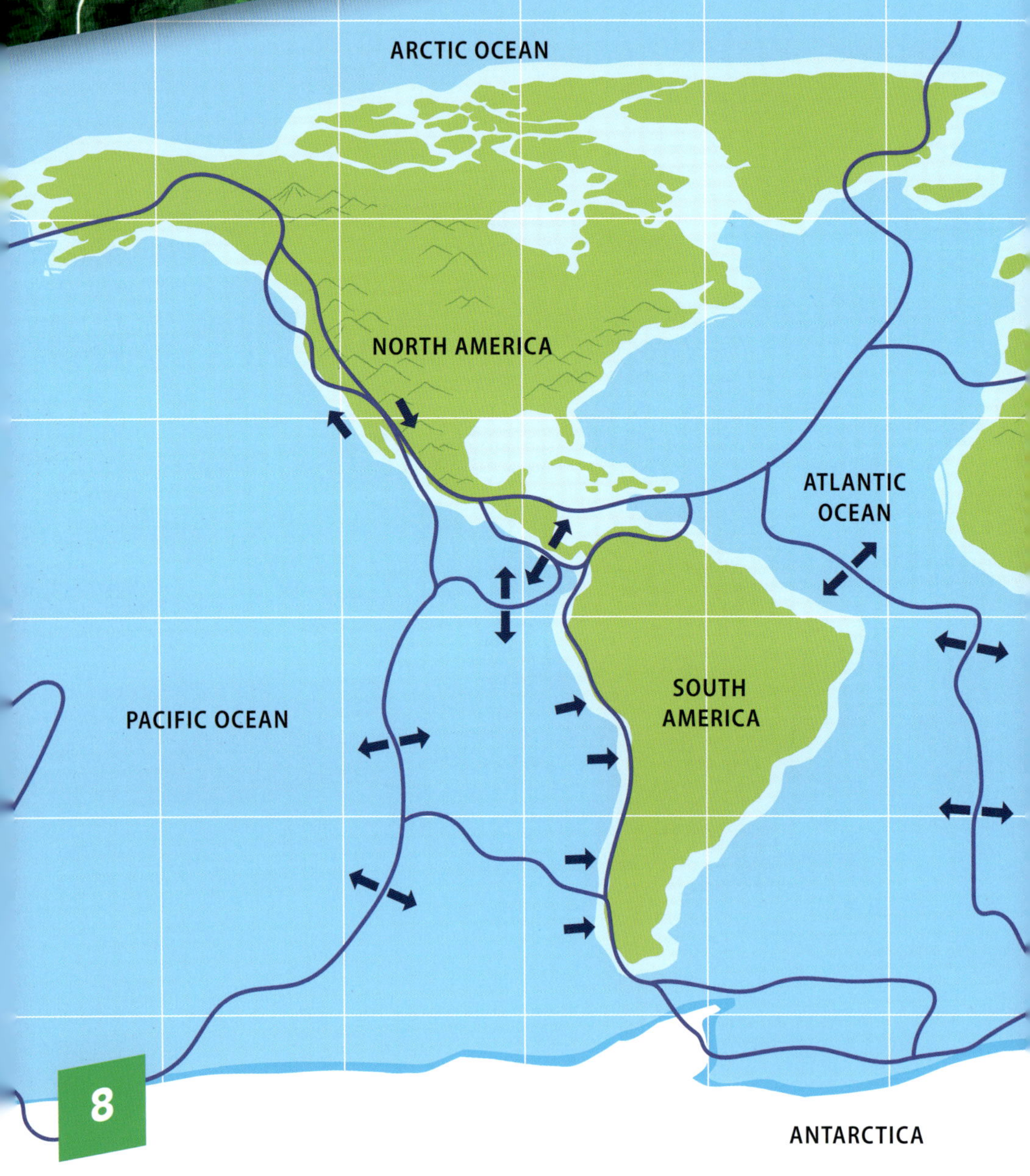

Earth's outer crust is made up of **plates**. These plates fit together like puzzle pieces. Where they meet is called a fault line.

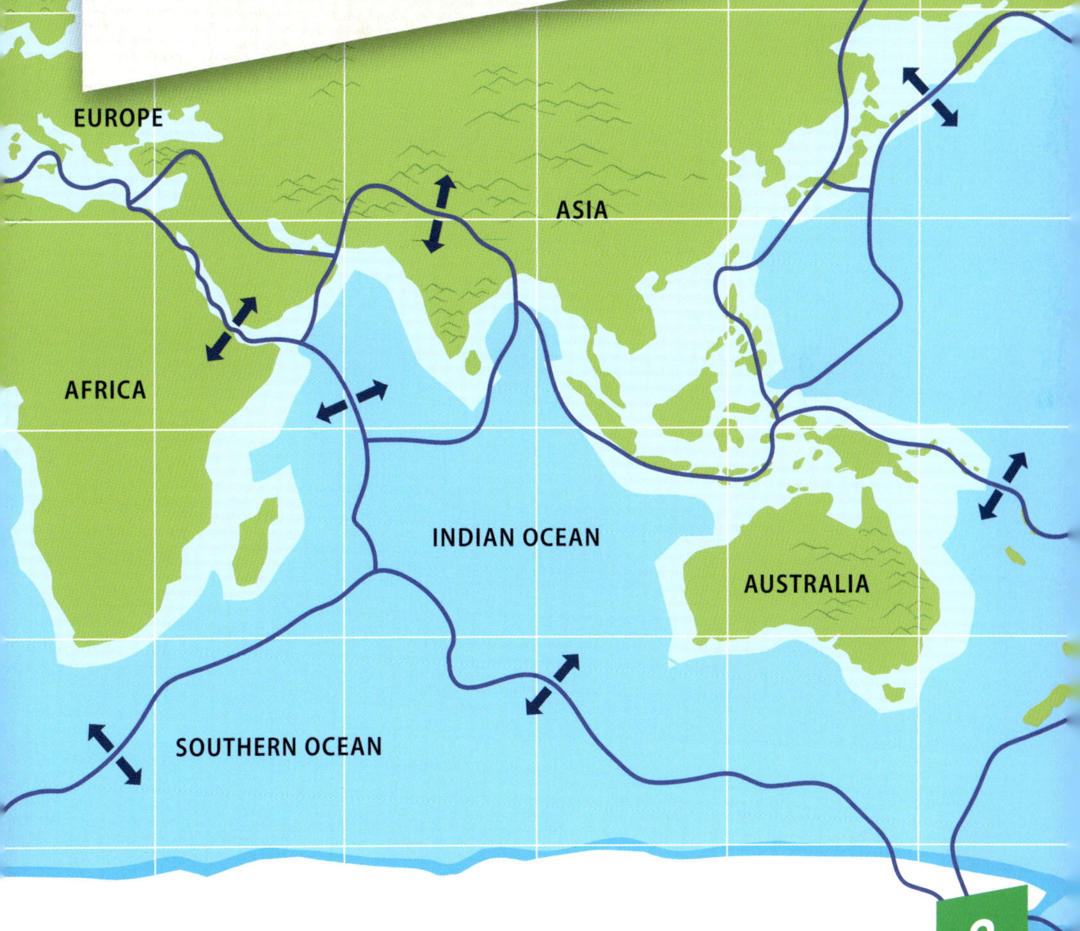

The Ring of Fire is a horseshoe-shaped belt made up of fault lines. It runs 25,000 miles (40,234 km) along the rim of the Pacific Ocean. More than 80% of earthquakes occur in this area.

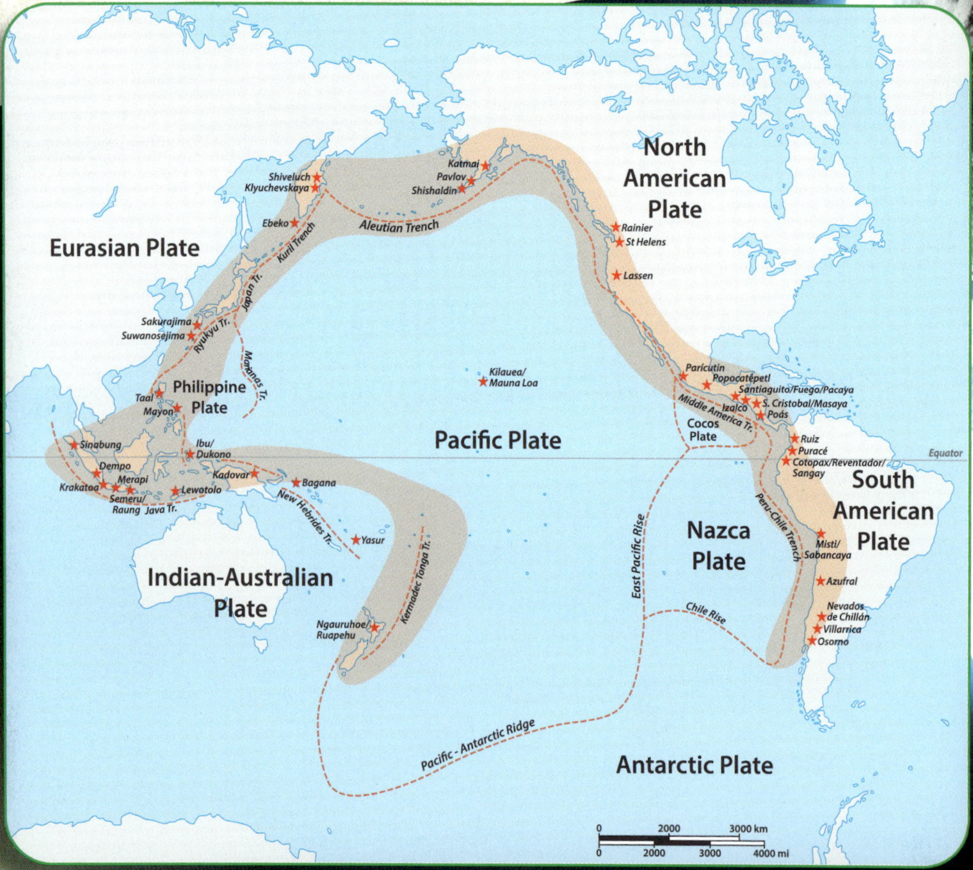

Earthquakes are caused by **plate** movement. When plates move or shift they can collide. This causes earthquakes.

Plates can move so much that they cause the landscape to change!

14

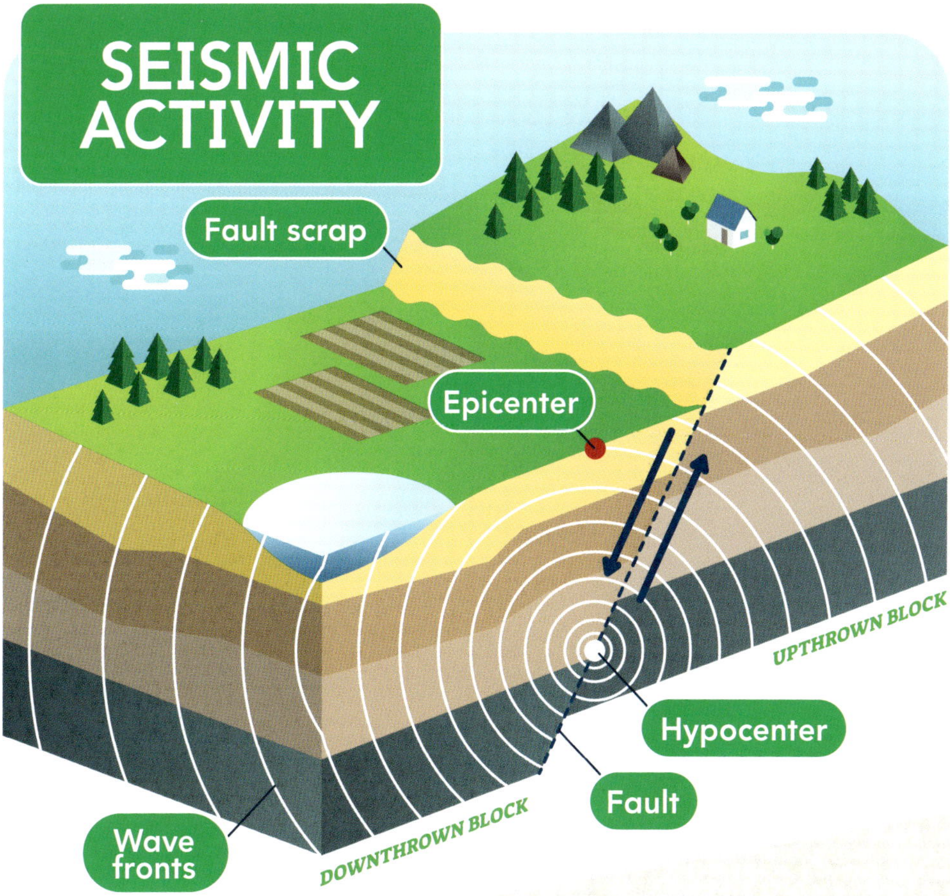

The hypocenter is where an earthquake occurs. **Seismic waves** travel outward from this point. The epicenter is above the hypocenter on the Earth's surface. This is where the effects are felt the most.

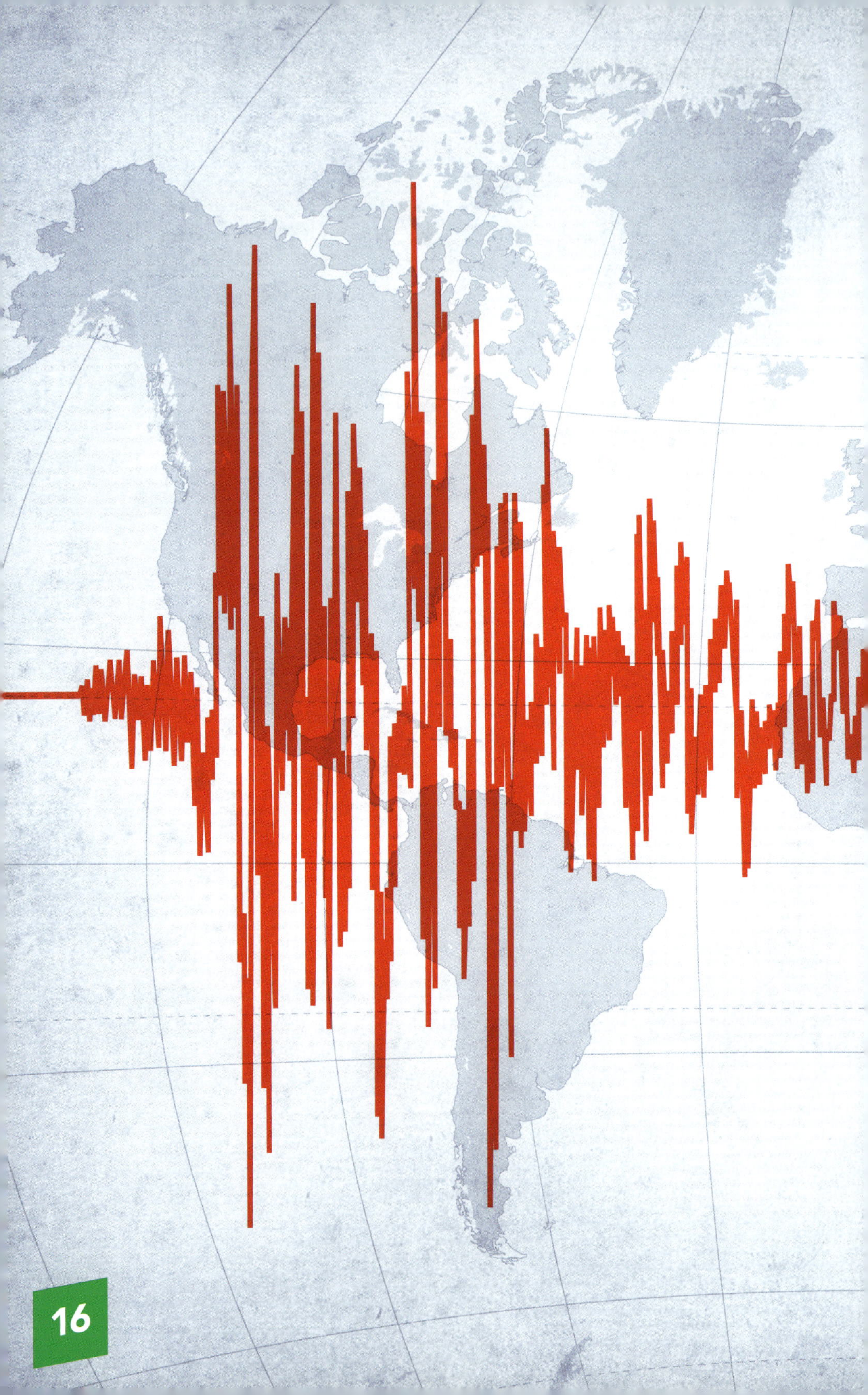

Earthquake Magnitude Scale

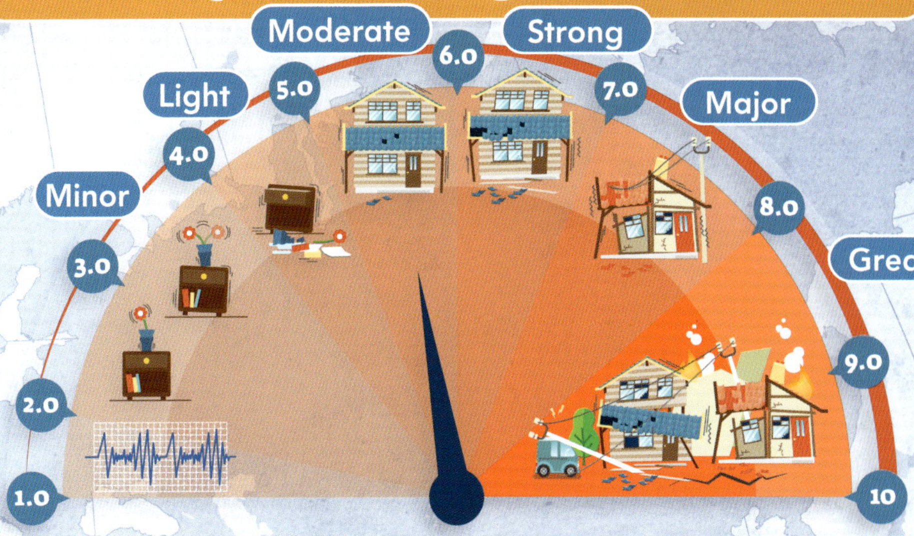

Tools can measure and record earthquakes. A seismograph detects and records seismic waves. Scientists can locate the epicenter using this data. A Richter scale measures an earthquake's strength.

Effects

Earthquakes can cause buildings and bridges to crack or crumble. They can split open roads too. Sometimes gas and power lines break. This can cause fires.

Earthquakes can lead to other natural disasters. Avalanches, landslides, and **tsunamis** can all be **triggered** by an earthquake.

More Facts

- Earthquakes cost the United States an estimated $14.7 billion in damage each year.
- The largest recorded earthquake in the US was in 1964. It measured 9.2 on the Richter scale. It happened in Prince William Sound, Alaska.
- Many buildings today are built to withstand earthquakes. They can sway or roll when the ground moves. This keeps them from **collapsing**.

Glossary

collapsing – falling down or caving in.

plate – also called a tectonic plate, one of the parts of the outer layer of planet Earth.

seismic wave – a vibration in the earth produced by an earthquake or other similar event.

triggered – caused or set off.

tsunami – a very large, often destructive, sea wave that is caused by an earthquake or explosion of a volcano under the ocean.

Index

Online Resources

Booklinks
NONFICTION NETWORK
FREE! ONLINE NONFICTION RESOURCES

To learn more about Earthquakes, please visit **abdobooklinks.com** or scan this QR code. These links are routinely monitored and updated to provide the most current information available.